Professor Bumblebrain's
Bonkers
Book on...
CREATION

This book is presented to

Theo Burrows

From the Bedford Salvation Army

"God bless you and keep you…"

Numbers 6:24

Published 2011 by CWR, Waverley Abbey House, Waverley Lane, Farnham, Surrey GU9 8EP, UK. Registered Charity No. 294387. Registered Limited Company No. 1990308.

See back of book for list of National Distributors.

Editing, design and production by CWR

Printed in China by 1010 Printing International

ISBN: 978-1-85345-622-0

Professor Bumblebrain's
Bonkers
Book on...
CREATION

ANDY ROBB

CWR

Good day, young reader. Welcome to my excellent and entertaining book, *Professor Bumblebrain's Bonkers Book on ... Creation*. You are probably thinking that to say such a thing is rather boastful and presumptuous.

Not so!

If you have read any of my other books then you will be well aware that I have a brain the size of a large cabbage and thus I am more than qualified to judge what is good and what is not, thank you very much.

You are no doubt wondering why I am presenting this book from within the grounds of a zoo.
IT HAD CROSSED MY MIND.
The reason is quite simple. I have had quite enough of sitting in my stuffy office and so, for this book, I have decided to go out and about.
Very fitting for a book on creation don't you think?
IF YOU SAY SO!

In this book we are going to examine some different points of view people have about how the world we live in was made.
ONE OF THESE VIEWS IS THE BELIEF THAT THE WORLD (AND EVERYTHING ON IT) WAS SET IN MOTION BY SOMETHING CALLED THE ...
BIG BANG!

... and has then evolved over billions of years to become what it is today.

Another widely held belief is that it was God who created everything and that the world may not be as old as some believe.
LIONS
APES

And, then again, there are those who believe that the world was created by God but who accept that in *some* areas of life evolution has taken place over time. In fact, young reader, there are possibly as many different views as stars in the sky so, to make it easier for us, we'll just concentrate on one or two.

In life there are many things that people disagree on, such as …
HOW MANY TIMES HAVE I TOLD YOU? DON'T EAT YOUR PEAS FROM THE WRONG SIDE OF THE FORK!
SAYS WHO?

HE'S THE BEST LOOKING OF THE LOT!
NO, HE'S NOT! HE IS!
RIP!

LET'S PAINT THE WALL BLUE.
NO WAY! IT'S YELLOW OR NOTHING!

But there's one thing that gets some people *really* hot under the collar – and that's the thorny question of who (or what) made the world …

GRRR! LOOKING AT YOU IT'S EASY TO SEE WHY YOU THINK THAT GOD MADE THE WORLD'S FIRST MAN FROM A PILE OF DIRT!
GRRR! LOOKING AT YOU MAKES IT EASY TO BELIEVE PEOPLE ARE DESCENDED FROM APES!

Not very pleasant, is it?

I trust that this book will help you come to your own conclusions, young person, and without falling out with me along the way. There will be no squabbling while I am around – is that clear?

LOUD AND!
GOOD.

As we have just seen, there are some people who believe that we human beings are distant relatives of the jolly old ape …

… but we will first need to travel back into the dim and distant past to find out precisely *why* they have come to that rather interesting conclusion.

uncle Bob

One thing that most people *can* agree on though is that once upon a time there was absolutely nothing. What do I mean by this? Well simply that the universe in which we all live once didn't exist. Should you have wished to post a letter to somebody such as myself and addressed it like so …

… you simply would not have been able to do so because there was, in fact, no universe.

We have no actual proof of this because there's nobody around today who was present at the time – not even your parents, as old as you might think they are.

What some clever people believe (though obviously not as brainy as yours truly) is that approximately 13 billion years ago the universe began and to be more precise, it began from nothing.

This is called **the Big Bang theory**.

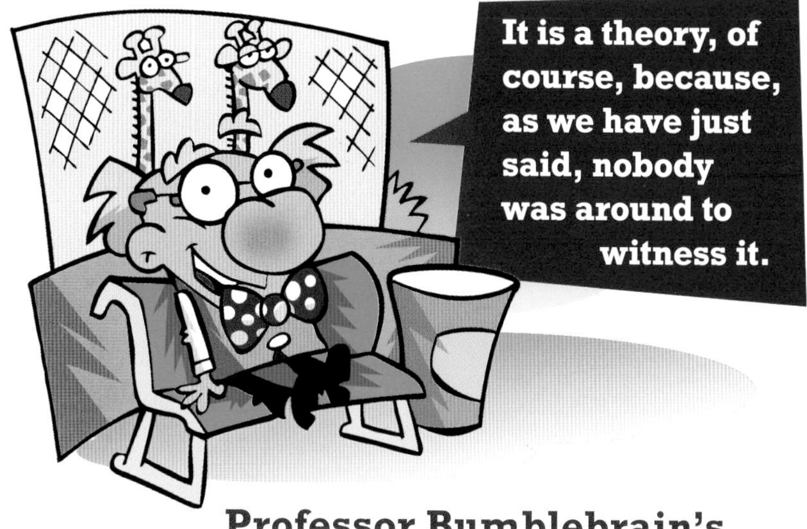

It is a theory, of course, because, as we have just said, nobody was around to witness it.

Professor Bumblebrain's Information Station ...

One billion is actually one thousand million and looks like this when written in numerals ...

1,000,000,000

So one thing that just about everyone seems to be agreed on is that our universe did indeed have a beginning.

The Big Bang theory is the notion that the universe started from a single point (a beginning) and has been expanding ever since, rather like a balloon that is steadily being blown up.

One remaining puzzle about this is where exactly this Big Bang came from in the first place ...

WHERE DID *THAT* COME FROM?

BANG!

... and, more to the point, *why* it happened.

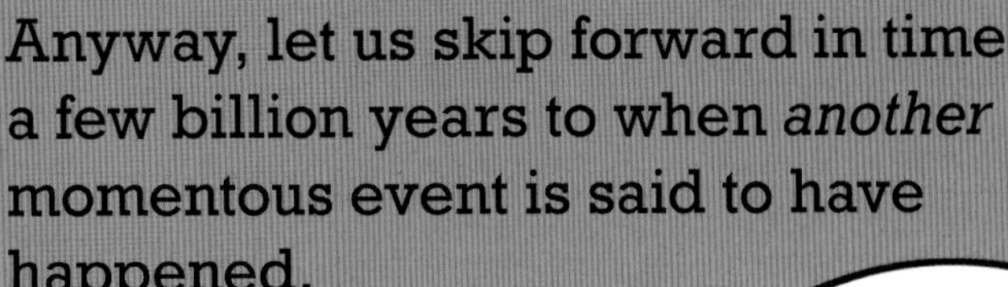

Anyway, let us skip forward in time a few billion years to when *another* momentous event is said to have happened.

A FEW BILLION YEARS? SLOW DOWN! WHAT'S THE RUSH?

It is believed by some that around 8.5 billion years after this Big Bang (that's about 4.5-ish billion years ago) planet Earth was formed.

But how, you may ask, did it actually happen? Well, evolutionists simply put it down to a whole load of space dust and gas joining forces – and the rest is history.

Over time this molten ball of gas cooled down and solidified, and then, just 4 billion years later (give or take), the jolly place was ready for plant life to begin to grow. How cool was that. Pardon the pun, dear reader. (Sometimes I simply cannot seem to help myself with my intelligent humour.)

The world then had another extremely long wait before anything that even closely resembled a human being showed up.
YAWN! THIS LONG WAIT IS SO BORING!
What evolutionists believe is that there were ape-like creatures roaming this planet and that we are descended from them.

They say that human-like creatures that stood upright (like we do) …

… didn't appear until just 2.5 million years ago, which is still a long time ago, as far as you and I are concerned, but is a drop in the ocean when it comes to the supposed age of the earth.

A boy is walking down the street and he sees a penguin merrily waddling along. He promptly finds a policeman who advises the lad to take the creature to the zoo.
The next day, to his surprise, the policeman discovers the boy walking down the street with the same penguin.
'I thought I told you to take that penguin to the zoo,' said the policeman.
'I did,' said the boy, 'and he really enjoyed it. Today I'm taking him to the cinema.'

Anyway, back to us being descended from apes.
Now I guess that if that *were* the case, and if over hundreds of thousands (even millions) of years ape-like creatures had evolved (or changed) into humans, then there would have to be plenty of bones of those that had died buried in the ground somewhere.

And what you would *also* expect to see from these bones would be evidence of how these ape-like creatures had changed, little by little over time, into human beings.

Although there have been odd bits of skull, jaw bones and teeth discovered which people have suggested prove this theory, it is, to be perfectly frank, rather flimsy evidence.

There has even been the odd hoax or two along the way where bits of human bones were sneakily joined to animal bones because people were so keen to convince everyone that we are descended from apes.
OI!

And now for the other side of the story.
As I have already told you, if you have being paying close attention, there are people who believe that the universe *didn't* come about by chance but that it came about on purpose.

To find out what these people think about this we will need to head straight for the Bible to find out what *it* has to say on the matter.

I'M HEADING STRAIGHT FOR THE BIBLE!
Bible
TRIP!

Most of what we are going to look at comes from the very first book of the Bible, which is called Genesis.
For your added information the Bible consists of 66 books. It's like your very own mini-library of everything to do with God.
SSSHHH!
I THINK YOU'RE TAKING THIS LIBRARY THING A BIT TOO FAR!
Bible

Genesis was also the name of a very famous rock band but you are obviously far too young to know about that, unless of course you're an adult who is sneakily reading this book hoping that nobody will catch you.
OOPS!
Adult caught in the act of sneakily reading this book

The Bible book Genesis has a rather different take on how our universe came into being and it all began with God speaking. It may surprise you that it was nothing more dramatic than that but, as far as God is concerned, words have *power*.

The Bible tells us that at the very *beginning* of time God set about the business of creating the universe. What the Bible *doesn't* tell us is how long God spent planning the whole thing, but it is a fair guess that He had given it quite a bit of thought considering how well it turned out.

Genesis says that for six full days God commanded things to happen and for six full days they did.
WHAT SORT OF THINGS?
I will tell you.

Day 1

First up, out of absolutely nowhere, the universe, the Earth, light (and darkness) all instantly appeared. No email announcements, no warnings on the radio, no text alerts. One minute there was nothing and the next minute stuff was appearing all over the place. God had simply said the words, 'Let there be light,' and … KABOOM! … there light was.

Just like that!

Day 2

Next up, God separated the Earth from outer space by creating sky which He slipped neatly between the two to make it possible for life to exist on our planet.

Day 3

On the third day God decided to make the world a more pleasant place in which to live. Jolly decent of Him, don't you think? Up until then the world was really little more than a big ball of watery wetness – but not for long. With a word of command God did a bit of clever tweaking to His handiwork so that there were now dry bits as well as wet bits. The dry bits were obviously called land and the wet bits were called the sea.

Now that there was land to grow things on God could set about adding greenery, such as plants, trees and flowers – and not forgetting yummy crops, fruit and vegetables for us to eat.

Day 4

Although the Bible says that there was already night-time and daytime at this point, God wanted to make sure that we could tell the difference between the two. So He created the sun to give us light during the day and the moon to act as a handy, soft glowing night-light.

How considerate is that? To top it all off, and to pretty things up, God splattered the night sky with more stars than you could care to count – though don't let me stop you having a go, should you so wish.

YOU'RE RIGHT. I'VE ALREADY RUN OUT OF FINGERS.

Day 5

As the week wore on God was really getting into His stride. With everything in place it was now time for Him to fill the skies and the sea with birds and fish. You name it, if it could fly or swim, God brought it into being on the fifth day of creation.

Day 6

Not to be left out, now it was time for the dry land to have some living creatures of its very own.
THAT'S A SHAME. I WAS ENJOYING HAVING THE PLACE TO OURSELVES.

From dinosaurs to dingoes,

pigs to pandas,

ants to aardvarks,

each and every kind of land-based creature was created by God on this one day.
And that was that!

Phew! What a busy week it had been for God. Must be time for Him to take a well-earned break and to put His feet up. Not quite yet. There was just one small but very important thing missing.

THERE WERE NO PEOPLE!

WHO'S BOTHERED?

Fret not, young reader! God had been saving the best until last. Although the Earth (and the universe in which it sits) must have brought God great pleasure, He hadn't quite finished the job. All of this had just been by way of preparation to provide the pride and joy of His creation with a place in which to live.

God hadn't just wanted a universe that was nice for Him to look at, enjoyable as that might have been.

God wanted to create something that He could talk to, something He could spend time with, something He could love and also something that would love Him back. And that *something* (if you hadn't guessed it already) …
I HAD!
… was people.

But when it came to making human beings, God decided to do things a little differently. Instead of using words like He'd done with everything else, this time around God opted for a more hands-on approach.

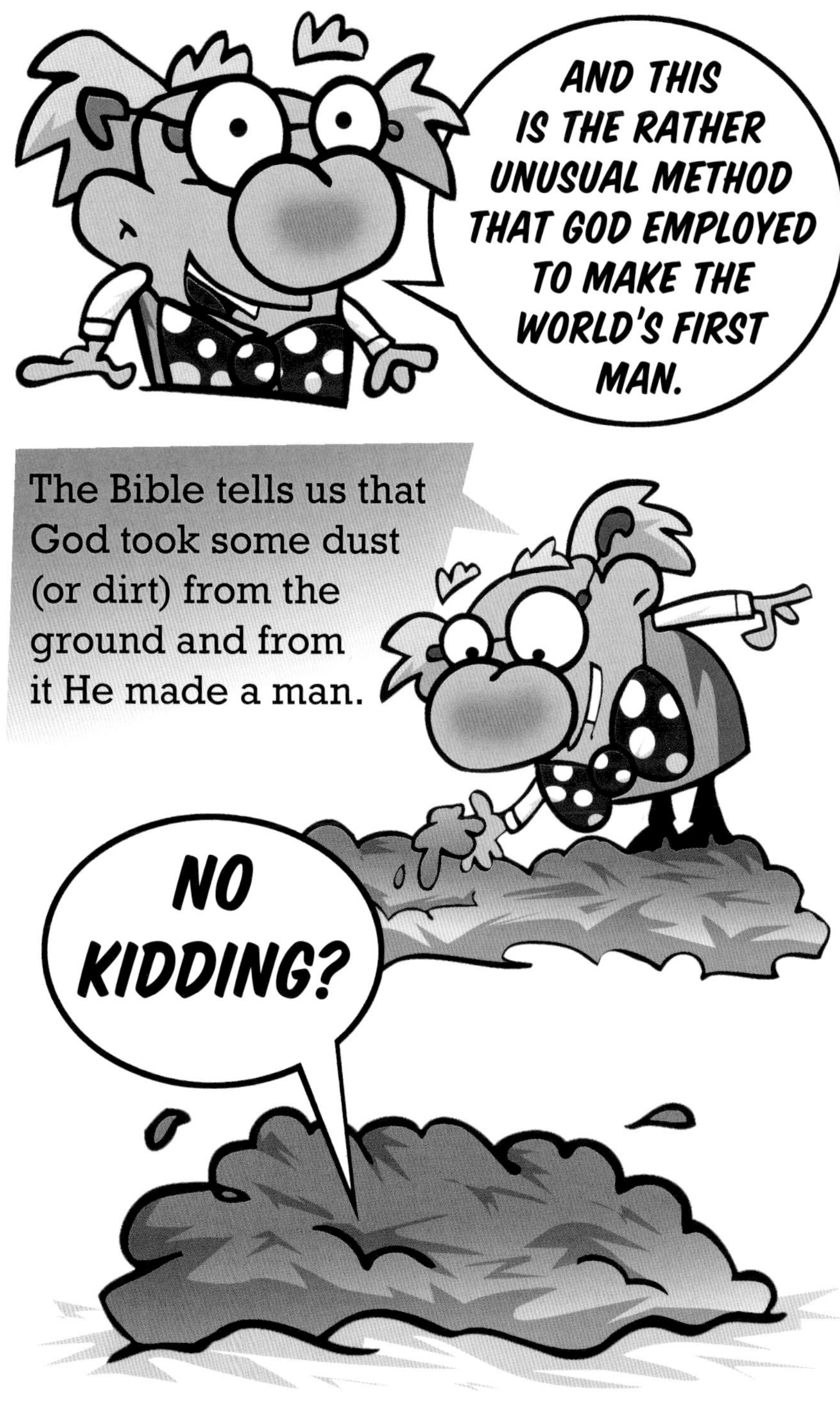

The Bible tells us that God took some dust (or dirt) from the ground and from it He made a man.

NO KIDDING?

No kidding. But a man made out of mud is really not much use to anyone is he?
WIPE YOUR FEET!
What I mean is that mud doesn't have any life in it. It's just a lifeless lump of wet dirt.
HEY, NOW YOU'RE GETTING PERSONAL!

So God breathed *His* life into the nostrils of the mud man and ...
DA DAH!
... the man sprung to life. Wow!
ACTUALLY, THINKING ABOUT IT, THIS IS MUCH BETTER, THANKS. I'M JUST NOT VERY GOOD WITH CHANGE.

As if *that* wasn't unusual enough, now take a look at what happened next.

God knew that the world was going to be a rather lonely place for the world's first man. He knew that what he really needed was a best buddy.

There's no doubt whatsoever that the animals God had made were an awesome bunch, but to be totally honest you wouldn't really want to spend your spare time hanging out with them.

I SAID, 'NICE WEATHER FOR THE TIME OF YEAR'. OH, NEVER MIND. YOU CAN'T HEAR A WORD I'M SAYING WITH A NECK THAT LONG.

THAT'S THE LAST TIME I PLAY FOOTBALL WITH YOU. I CAN'T AFFORD TO KEEP BUYING NEW FOOTBALLS ALL THE TIME!
BANG!
BEING INVITED ROUND FOR DINNER BY A DUNG BEETLE HAS TO BE THE WORST!

Fortunately for Adam (which is the name God gave the man) God was on his case.
THAT'S GOOD NEWS!
First of all there was the small matter of God whipping out one of Adam's ribs so that He could make Adam a companion from it.
THAT'S BAD NEWS!

Fear not, God put Adam into a deep sleep before performing surgery on the fellow.
PHEW! THAT'S A RELIEF ...
ZZZZZ

While Adam was in the Land of Nod God took out one of his ribs from which He made him a wife. How kind!

And so, with Day 6 of creation drawing to a close, God handed over the responsibility of looking after the world that He had so lovingly created to Adam and his wife (who was called Eve).
ER, IS THERE AN INSTRUCTION BOOK FOR THIS PLACE?

Finally, on the seventh and final day of creation the Bible says that God rested. Not that God was tired, of course, because God never gets tired. He's God after all. But God rested just because His work was complete and everything that needed to be created had been. It was a job well done.

For your information, young reader, there is some debate over whether these were actually normal 24-hour days like you and I know them or whether they were, in fact, very long periods as the Hebrew word used for 'day' also has the meaning of 'unspecified time period' or 'age'.

One thing's for sure, however long it took, those who believe in God's work of creation will all agree that the end result was absolutely fantasmagorical.

Probably the reason some people think that they couldn't have been normal length days is because the notion of creating the whole world in just six days sounds completely ridiculous.

SIX DAYS TO MAKE THE WORLD? DON'T MAKE ME LAUGH!

Who could possibly do all of that in such a short space of time? Well, God certainly could: but exactly how long He took is not very easy to know for sure.

Just as an added thought, the Bible says that each of these days had an evening ...
... and a morning, and as far as I can see a long period of time doesn't have either of those.

That said, there are those who would say that the account in Genesis was written in a poetic style and that perhaps it wasn't all meant to be taken absolutely literally. What do you think?

Another sticking point that we perhaps need to touch upon before moving ahead is the age of our Earth. Or to put it another way, **how old is our jolly planet?**

As we have mentioned previously, some people believe that our world is millions and millions of years old.
The Bible, on the other hand, would seem to paint a somewhat different picture.

If you take the Bible account absolutely literally it would appear that the world's very first man was made just six days after the world was created and not millions of years later. But, then again, we read later in the Bible that with the Lord a day is like a thousand years! No easy answers here!

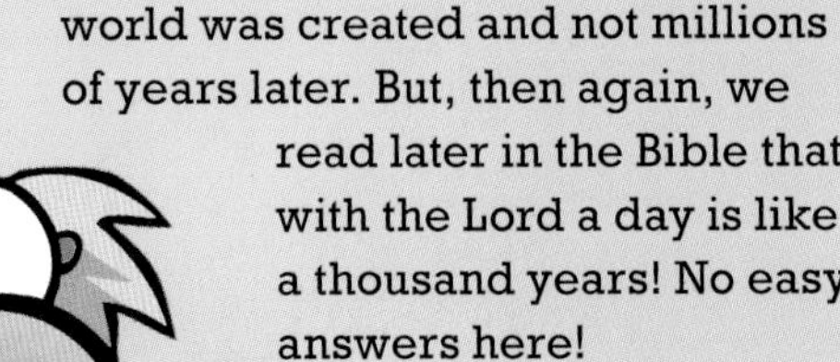

In Bible book Genesis (to which I referred earlier) there is a handy list of Adam's descendants and some handy info about when they were born.

For instance we can find out that Noah (of ark fame) was born 1,056 years after Adam.
Property of Adam
WHAT ON EARTH AM I GOING TO USE THIS HEIRLOOM FROM MY ANCESTOR ADAM FOR?

People have used these dates and ages to have a go at working out how old they think the world is.

What they've come up with is rather interesting ...
WHEN YOU PUT ALL THIS HANDY INFORMATION TOGETHER AND CRUNCH THE NUMBERS LIKE SO ...
6,000
... WHAT YOU GET IS A FIGURE OF AROUND ONLY 6,000 YEARS AS THE AGE OF THE EARTH, FROM THE BEGINNING OF CREATION UNTIL THE PRESENT DAY.
Are you sure? I thought I was much older than that.

As I say, this is what *some* people think. Whilst I have my own opinion on these matters, it is important to investigate and talk to people to help you think this through for yourself. This leads us on rather nicely to another interesting piece of the puzzle.
WHAT HAPPENED TO THE DINOSAURS?
Precisely!
THAT'S A VERY GOOD QUESTION!
DINOSAUR

I do hope that you are finding this presentation interesting and that my superior intelligence is not bamboozling you too much, young reader.
ER, WHAT DOES BAMBOOZLING MEAN?

Let me continue.

In a nutshell, evolutionists are of the firm opinion that dinosaurs came on to the scene approximately 235 million years ago, and way, way before human beings existed.

They say that dinosaurs ran the show on planet Earth until a rather unfortunate cataclysmic disaster wiped the lot of them off the face of the Earth somewhere around 65 million years ago.

WE'VE BEEN ON THIS PLANET ABOUT 170 MILLION YEARS. LOOKS LIKE WE'RE HERE TO STAY!

Professor Bumblebrain's Information Station ...

Probably the first discovery of what we now call dinosaurs was in 1677 when a gentleman called Dr Robert Plot found some large bones that he at first believed belonged to a giant elephant or a giant human but eventually proved otherwise. The name 'dinosaur' wasn't coined until 1842 and it actually comes from the Greek word meaning 'terrible lizard'.
BUT I'M A NICE LIZARD.

There are also those who have a very different take on this whole dinosaur debate.

As far as they are concerned dinosaurs were around right at the very beginning of creation when the Bible says that God made every living creature. This would have obviously included dinosaurs.

Because everyone (including people) were vegetarians way back then there would have been no problem for humans and dinosaurs to live side by side …
… and without the fear that these mahoosive beasts would gobble them up for a breakfast.
SNAP!

It is thought that dinosaurs simply became extinct like so many other species of creatures

So, who is right? Is it simply one or the other? Or might a process of evolution have occurred within creation itself? For the time being it remains a mystery. Some questions for us to ponder …

Dinosaur
R.I.P
WHAT WE CAN DO IS EXPLORE A LITTLE BIT MORE AND SEE IF THAT HELPS.

For your information, there are fascinating tales of dinosaur-like creatures throughout history (and even in the Bible) but for now I want to look at the evidence we have that dinosaurs once walked this earth.

The main clues we have are from fossilised dinosaurs that have been discovered around the world.

WHAT IS A FOSSIL, YOU MAY ASK?

I MIGHT, BUT THEN AGAIN I MIGHT NOT!

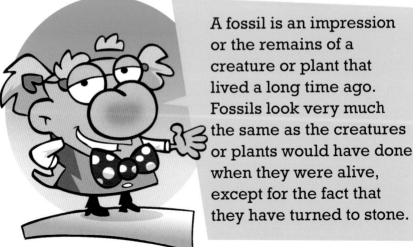

A fossil is an impression or the remains of a creature or plant that lived a long time ago. Fossils look very much the same as the creatures or plants would have done when they were alive, except for the fact that they have turned to stone.

How exactly is a fossil formed you may ask?

OK. HOW EXACTLY IS A FOSSIL FORMED?

BECAUSE I AM IN A PARTICULARLY HELPFUL MOOD, I WILL TELL YOU.

THANKS!

The most common way that a fossil is formed is when a creature or a plant dies and is then covered with mud, sand or soil. Minerals are gradually absorbed into the skeleton, which then harden.
Over time the surrounding mud and soil also hardens until it eventually becomes rock – and thus the creature or plant is preserved for all time.

NOW FOR THE TRICKY BIT ...

This process has to happen really quickly, before the thing that has been buried in mud completely disintegrates. This means that for something as large as a dinosaur to become fossilised it needs to be buried pretty sharpish.

There is an outside chance that this could happen if the poor creature was out for a swim and drowned (presuming dinosaurs could swim) ...

The problem this poses is that many of the fossilised animals that have been unearthed lived all their time on land. So the question we have to ask is: how could they possibly get embedded in mud, sand or soil fast enough for the fossilisation process to work?

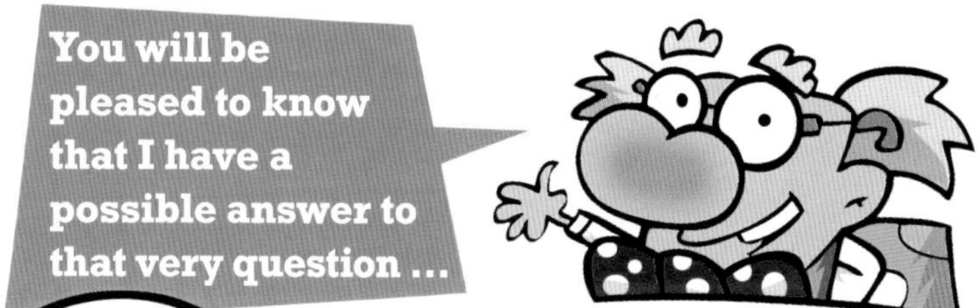

You will be pleased to know that I have a possible answer to that very question ...

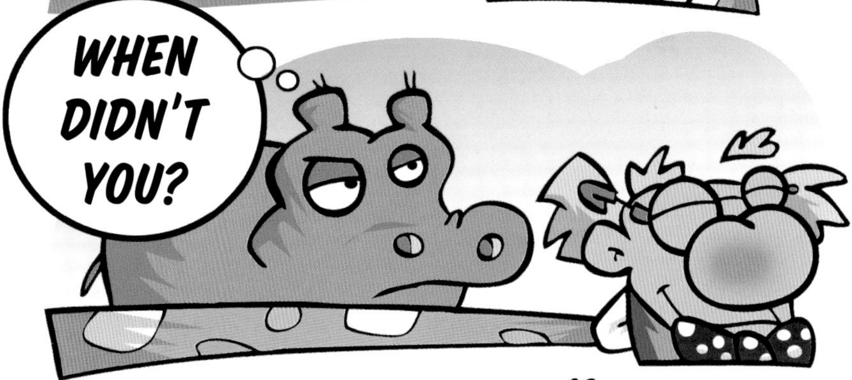

WHEN DIDN'T YOU?

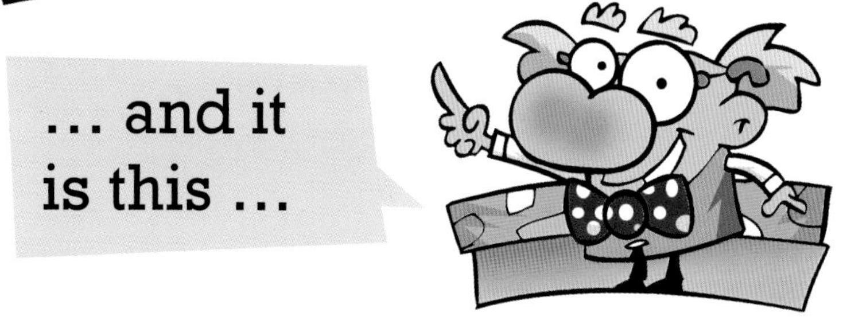

... and it is this ...

In the Bible there is a story that most of you have probably heard of. It is all about a chap called Noah and a big, box-like boat called an ark. To cut a long story short, God was well and truly cheesed off with the human race because they had turned out (in the main) to be a wicked bunch.

GRRR! WHO'RE YOU CALLING WICKED!

God decided to call time on the whole thing and to wipe them from the face of the Earth with a ferocious flood. The Bible says that He regretted ever making humans.

Fear not! All was not completely lost. There was one person who had kept himself in God's good books and that was good old Noah. And when I say old, I mean old. Noah had clocked up a respectable 600 years by the time he'd finished building the ark.

Noah was the one good guy left so God spared him, along with his whole family.

HE'S NOT SUCH A BAD DAD AFTER ALL!

God told Noah to build the ark …

WHY DOES EVERYTHING COME IN KIT FORM NOWADAYS?
Build Your Own ark Kit

When it finally arrived, the flood destroyed every living thing on the face of the Earth. As the waters raged around the globe the sea would have been a swirling torrent of mud, sand, soil, dead plants and animals.

AS THE WATERS FINALLY SETTLED AND THE FLOOD CEASED, EVERY LIVING THING WOULD HAVE BEEN BURIED IN THIS MUDDY MIXTURE.

If this was indeed what happened then archaeologists could expect to stumble across the evidence in the course of their excavations.
And sure enough they have!

OOPS! I'VE STUMBLED ACROSS EVIDENCE OF A FLOOD IN THE COURSE OF MY EXCAVATIONS.
TRIP!

Right around the world, massive fossil graveyards have been found containing the fossilised remains of thousands upon thousands of dead animals, and all apparently buried in a short space of time.

WHILE YOU ARE EXPANDING YOUR BRAIN BY PUZZLING OVER THESE INTERESTING DISCOVERIES, IT IS WORTH NOTING THAT THE BIBLE TALKS ABOUT BIG BEASTS THAT LIVED ONLY A FEW THOUSAND YEARS AGO BUT WHICH SEEM TO BEAR AN UNCANNY RESEMBLANCE TO ONES WE KNOW AND LOVE.
Bible

Once such Bible story features a whopper of a beast called a Behemoth.

First I would like you to read the Bible bit ...
AWW! NOT READING!
... and then grab yourself a pen and paper and have a go at drawing a picture of the creature from the description. You may be surprised at the results ...!
I'M NOT VERY GOOD AT THIS KIND OF THING, PROFESSOR BUMBLEBRAIN.

Does your drawing resemble a dinosaur? If it does then maybe these fabled beasts weren't living as long ago as some would have us believe.

HERE IS THE DESCRIPTION TAKEN FROM BIBLE BOOK JOB, CHAPTER 40 AND VERSES 15–19.

'LOOK AT BEHEMOTH, WHICH I MADE ALONG WITH YOU AND WHICH FEEDS ON GRASS LIKE AN OX. WHAT STRENGTH IT HAS IN ITS LOINS, WHAT POWER IN THE MUSCLES OF ITS BELLY! ITS TAIL SWAYS LIKE A CEDAR; THE SINEWS OF ITS THIGHS ARE CLOSE-KNIT. ITS BONES ARE TUBES OF BRONZE, ITS LIMBS LIKE RODS OF IRON. IT RANKS FIRST AMONG THE WORKS OF GOD, YET ITS MAKER CAN APPROACH IT WITH HIS SWORD.'

It is true that some people say that the creature described must have been a hippopotamus or an elephant, but do they have a tail like a cedar tree?
WHAT DID HAVE A TAIL THAT BIG WAS THE BRACHIOSAURUS.
FOOD FOR THOUGHT EH, YOUNG READER?

HOW ARE WE DOING FOR TIME?

HMM, WE'RE OK.

Looking at my splendid watch reminds me of another important difference of opinion between people when it comes to all this stuff about when and how the world was created.

My watch is a clever and intricate piece of mechanical engineering on which I rely to tell me the time of day.
This particular watch has the name of the maker slap bang in the middle of the watch face, lest anyone should think for one moment that it came about of its own accord.

Aha, you may say that, but this is precisely where people fall out with each other. The question that causes people to get so aggie (an expression that I gather is quite popular with you youngsters) with each other is whether our world actually has a maker or whether it doesn't.

Some people would say that the universe (and everything in it) began its life with the Big Bang that I told you about earlier in this book and from that moment all things have slowly evolved into what they are today.

They say that the chemicals that formed part of this beginning would have gradually formed into simple cells which then evolved into basic water-based creatures.

Over the millions of years that followed they changed into fish and then the fish morphed into amphibians (which are creatures that can live in water and on dry land) which then changed into four-legged animals, which then turned into apes and which finally turned into human beings.

AN INTERESTING THOUGHT, DON'T YOU THINK?

On the other hand, others believe that the universe (and everything in it) began its life with God and that He made everything the way it is right from the very start.
Fish were fish. Birds were birds. Apes were apes and people were people.

Very important point … Whether or not any process of evolution was involved, as far as I am concerned, human beings aren't a chance accident but are wonderfully designed creatures, made deliberately by God – in the same way that my watch was also designed and made by someone. Let's take a minute to look at just how amazing that design is …

Professor Bumblebrain's Fascinating Facts about Human Beings …

Our lungs inhale an estimated ten thousand litres of air every day.

GASP! COULD YOU SAVE SOME FOR ME?

SUCK!

Our brain is more complex than the most powerful computer and has (according to some people's calculations) over 100 billion nerve cells.

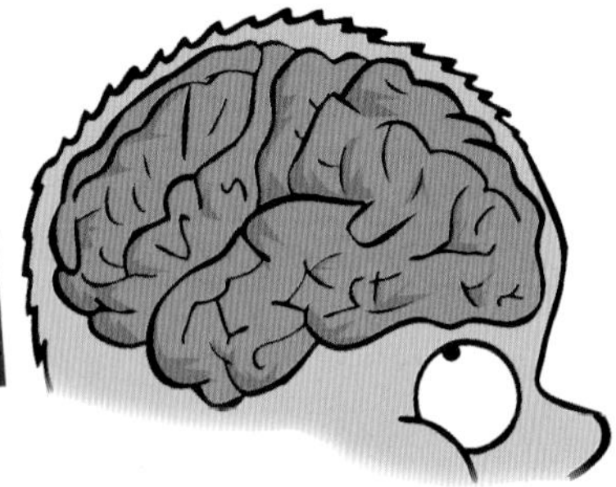

IT GOES WITHOUT SAYING THAT SOMEONE WITH A BRAIN THE SIZE OF MINE WILL HAVE CONSIDERABLY MORE.

Each cell in your body is estimated to have over 1 metre of DNA.

Someone has worked out that the total length of your circulatory system stretches an amazing 60,000 miles. That is more than twice the distance around the Earth.

In 1 square inch of skin ...

An attempt by the artist at drawing 1 square inch of skin! Not very good, is it?

... there are nerve fibres, pain sensors, nerve cells, heat sensors, nerve endings, metres of blood vessels and hundreds of sweat glands.

Our eyes can distinguish up to an estimated 1 million colour surfaces and take in more information than the largest telescope known to man.

Our hearing is so sensitive that it can distinguish between thousands of different sounds.

CRASH! TOOT!
PARP! BANG! BEEP!
BISH! BASH!

SO TRUE, PROFESSOR, BUT I WISH IT WASN'T!

HAVE YOU DONE YOUR HOMEWORK YET?

OUR SENSE OF TOUCH IS MORE REFINED THAN ANY DEVICE EVER CREATED.

Our nose is our personal air-conditioning system: it warms cold air, cools hot air and filters impurities.

People blink approximately once every four seconds. That's because the eyelids act as windscreen wipers, and the eyelashes help to keep dust and grime from getting into the eye itself.

Every tongue has its own individual print.

The big toe is actually one of the most important elements within the body, as it balances the skeleton and enables the owner to move forward when walking. Without it, we would simply fall over.

YOUR EYES ARE COMPOSED OF SOMEWHERE AROUND 2 MILLION WORKING PARTS.

IT IS IMPOSSIBLE TO SNEEZE WITH YOUR EYES OPEN.

YOUR EYES WILL FOCUS ON ABOUT 50 THINGS PER SECOND.

So, when you think about how amazing we human beings are, it is almost impossible to believe that there wasn't some clever creator behind it all, who designed us and then skilfully put us together.

IN FACT THAT IS PRECISELY WHAT BIBLE BOOK JEREMIAH, CHAPTER 1 AND VERSE 5, SAYS ...
'BEFORE I FORMED YOU IN THE WOMB I KNEW YOU.'

AND THEN
IN BIBLE BOOK
PSALMS (PRONOUNCED
'SARMS') PSALM
139 AND VERSE 13,
IT SAYS ...
'FOR YOU CREATED MY
INMOST BEING; YOU KNIT
ME TOGETHER IN MY
MOTHER'S WOMB.'
IT SEEMS TO
ME THAT GOD WANTS
US TO KNOW THAT WE ARE
NOT A CHANCE HAPPENING
BUT A WONDERFULLY CREATED
HUMAN BEING WITH WHOM
HE WANTS TO BE
FRIENDS.

BUT THE BIBLE DOESN'T STOP THERE. NOT ONLY DOES IT TELL US THAT THERE IS A GOD WHO MADE US, BUT IT ALSO TELLS US THAT THE WORLD AROUND US WAS HIS HANDIWORK.

In Bible book Romans, chapter 1 and verse 20, it says that '… since the creation of the world God's invisible qualities – his eternal power and divine nature – have been clearly seen …'.

Put simply it means that just like the watch I was talking about has a maker, so also does everything we see in nature – and the name of that maker is none other than God.

When you look up into the awesome night sky,

when you marvel at the way a chameleon changes colour,

when you see a field of corn, they all point to the fact that it was God who made them.

IT ALSO SAYS IN BIBLE BOOK PSALMS, PSALM 19 AND VERSES 1–4, THAT 'THE HEAVENS DECLARE THE GLORY OF GOD; THE SKIES PROCLAIM THE WORK OF HIS HANDS.
DAY AFTER DAY THEY POUR FORTH SPEECH;
NIGHT AFTER NIGHT THEY DISPLAY KNOWLEDGE.
THERE IS NO SPEECH OR LANGUAGE WHERE THEIR VOICE IS NOT HEARD.'

It is as if God is using nature to speak to all people, everywhere, to tell us, loud and clear, that He is there and that it was He who made it all.

The universe has been constructed with such precision that even the smallest of changes would cause the entire universe to fall apart.

But that is not all.

Scientists have also discovered that our planet is absolutely perfectly positioned in the universe to support life.

Just suppose someone wanted to move house …

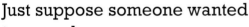

One of the things that would be near the top of their priority list would be where their home was going to be located, would it not?
FOR SALE
TO BE FAIR, IT DID SAY THAT IT HAD GOOD VIEWS!

The Earth is located just the right distance from our sun. If it were any *further* away from the sun we would all freeze.

If we were any *closer* it would be the reverse and we would burn to a cinder.

AM I IMAGINING IT OR IS IT GETTING WARM ROUND HERE?
FIZZLE!
NOPE, YOU'RE NOT IMAGINING IT!

Even the teensiest weensiest (a technical term which I hope does not baffle you) variation in our planet's distance from the sun would make life on Earth completely impossible.

Did you know?

The moon affects ocean tides which flow in and out so that the sea water doesn't stagnate. If the moon were just a tad nearer to us or a smidgeon further away from us the seas would flood the coastlines of our world.

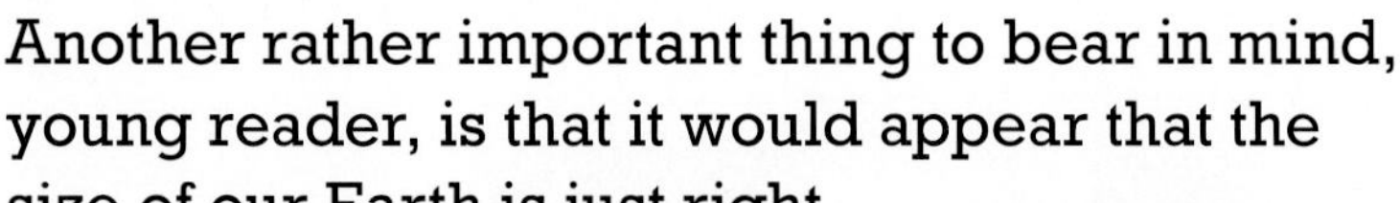

Another rather important thing to bear in mind, young reader, is that it would appear that the size of our Earth is just right.

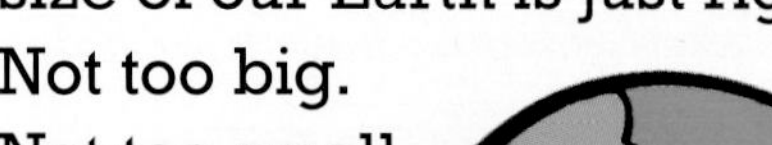

Not too big.
Not too small.

A LITTLE SMALLER AND THE EARTH'S ATMOSPHERE WHICH SUPPORTS LIFE WOULD NOT BE POSSIBLE.

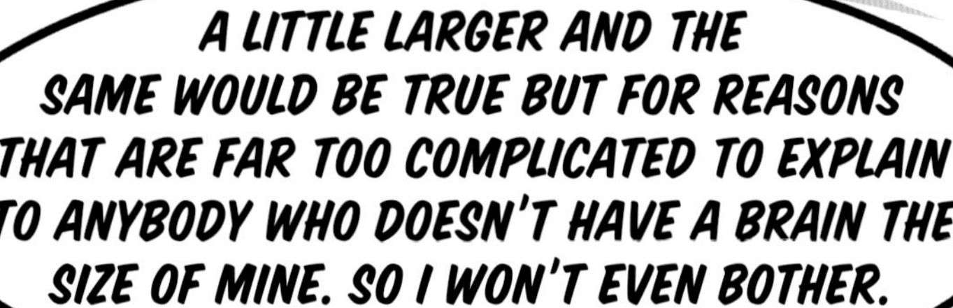

A LITTLE LARGER AND THE SAME WOULD BE TRUE BUT FOR REASONS THAT ARE FAR TOO COMPLICATED TO EXPLAIN TO ANYBODY WHO DOESN'T HAVE A BRAIN THE SIZE OF MINE. SO I WON'T EVEN BOTHER.

AS WE COME TO THE END OF ANOTHER OF MY FASCINATING AND THOUGHT-PROVOKING BOOKS, WE ARE LEFT WITH A VERY INTERESTING QUESTION: WILL WE EVER UNDERSTAND EXACTLY HOW OUR WONDERFUL, INTRICATE WORLD BEGAN?

EXIT

Whether it started with a 'Big Bang', was created in six days or over a much longer time, whether it evolved over millions of years or not, I find myself reaching the following conclusion: that it was **God** who made the universe and set the world within it as a wonderful home for the pinnacle of His creation: **human beings – of which you are one!**

But that's only my conclusion, young reader. What do you think?

A GOOD QUESTION!

Well, that's something for you to ponder. There are many questions and we won't have all the answers, but for now one thing is for sure. If God *did* make us then you and I must be very special for the Creator of the universe to have taken such care to make us who we are.

AND THAT, YOUNG READER, IS ALL I HAVE TO SAY ON THIS SUBJECT.

UNTIL WE MEET AGAIN. GOODBYE!
GOODBYE!
ZOO

National Distributors

UK: (and countries not listed below)
CWR, Waverley Abbey House, Waverley Lane, Farnham, Surrey GU9 8EP.
Tel: (01252) 784700 Outside UK (44) 1252 784700 Email: mail@cwr.org.uk

AUSTRALIA: KI Entertainment, Unit 21 317-321 Woodpark Road, Smithfield, New South Wales 2164.
Tel: 1 800 850 777 Fax: 02 9604 3699 Email: sales@kientertainment.com.au

CANADA: David C Cook Distribution Canada, PO Box 98, 55 Woodslee Avenue, Paris,
Ontario N3L 3E5. Tel: 1800 263 2664 Email: sandi.swanson@davidccook.ca

GHANA: Challenge Enterprises of Ghana, PO Box 5723, Accra. Tel: (021) 222437/223249
Fax: (021) 226227 Email: ceg@africaonline.com.gh

HONG KONG: Cross Communications Ltd, 1/F, 562A Nathan Road, Kowloon.
Tel: 2780 1188 Fax: 2770 6229 Email: cross@crosshk.com

INDIA: Crystal Communications, 10-3-18/4/1, East Marredpalli, Secunderabad – 500026, Andhra Pradesh.
Tel/Fax: (040) 27737145 Email: crystal_edwj@rediffmail.com

KENYA: Keswick Books and Gifts Ltd, PO Box 10242-00400, Nairobi.
Tel: (254) 20 312639/3870125 Email: keswick@swiftkenya.com

MALAYSIA: Canaanland, No. 25 Jalan PJU 1A/41B, NZX Commercial Centre, Ara Jaya, 47301 Petaling Jaya,
Selangor. Tel: (03) 7885 0540/1/2 Fax: (03) 7885 0545 Email: info@canaanland.com.my

Salvation Book Centre (M) Sdn Bhd, 23 Jalan SS 2/64, 47300 Petaling Jaya, Selangor.
Tel: (03) 78766411/78766797 Fax: (03) 78757066/78756360
Email: info@salvationbookcentre.com

NEW ZEALAND: KI Entertainment, Unit 21 317-321 Woodpark Road, Smithfield,
New South Wales 2164, Australia. Tel: 0 800 850 777 Fax: +612 9604 3699
Email: sales@kientertainment.com.au

NIGERIA: FBFM, Helen Baugh House, 96 St Finbarr's College Road, Akoka, Lagos.
Tel: (01) 7747429/4700218/825775/827264 Email: fbfm@hyperia.com

PHILIPPINES: OMF Literature Inc, 776 Boni Avenue, Mandaluyong City.
Tel: (02) 531 2183 Fax: (02) 531 1960 Email: gloadlaon@omflit.com

SINGAPORE: Alby Commercial Enterprises Pte Ltd, 95 Kallang Avenue #04-00, AIS Industrial Building, 339420.
Tel: (65) 629 27238 Fax: (65) 629 27235 Email: marketing@alby.com.sg

SOUTH AFRICA: Struik Christian Books, 80 MacKenzie Street, PO Box 1144, Cape Town 8000.
Tel: (021) 462 4360 Fax: (021) 461 3612 Email: info@struikchristianmedia.co.za

SRI LANKA: Christombu Publications (Pvt) Ltd, Bartleet House, 65 Braybrooke Place, Colombo 2.
Tel: (9411) 2421073/2447665 Email: dhanad@bartleet.com

USA: David C Cook Distribution Canada, PO Box 98, 55 Woodslee Avenue, Paris, Ontario N3L 3E5, Canada.
Tel: 1800 263 2664 Email: sandi.swanson@davidccook.ca

CWR is a Registered Charity - Number 294387
CWR is a Limited Company registered in England - Registration Number 1990308

IF YOU LIKED THIS BOOK YOU'LL LOVE THE BARMY PROFESSOR'S OTHER STORIES BY ANDY ROBB

Professor Bumblebrain's Bonkers Book on Bible Heroes
At the Professor's exciting award ceremony, The Bumblebrains, we're introduced to a star-studded line-up.
ISBN: 978-1-85345-578-0

Professor Bumblebrain's Bonkers Book on Jesus
Professor Bumblebrain introduces Jesus, to explain why He came to earth, His awesome miracles, His amazing part in God's rescue plan and how we can know Him today.
ISBN: 978-1-85345- 623-7

Professor Bumblebrain's Bonkers Book on God
Get the Professor's brainy answers to questions like:///// Who is God? What is He like? Where does He live? How can I get to know Him?
ISBN: 978-1-85345-579-7

100-page paperbacks, 129x197mm

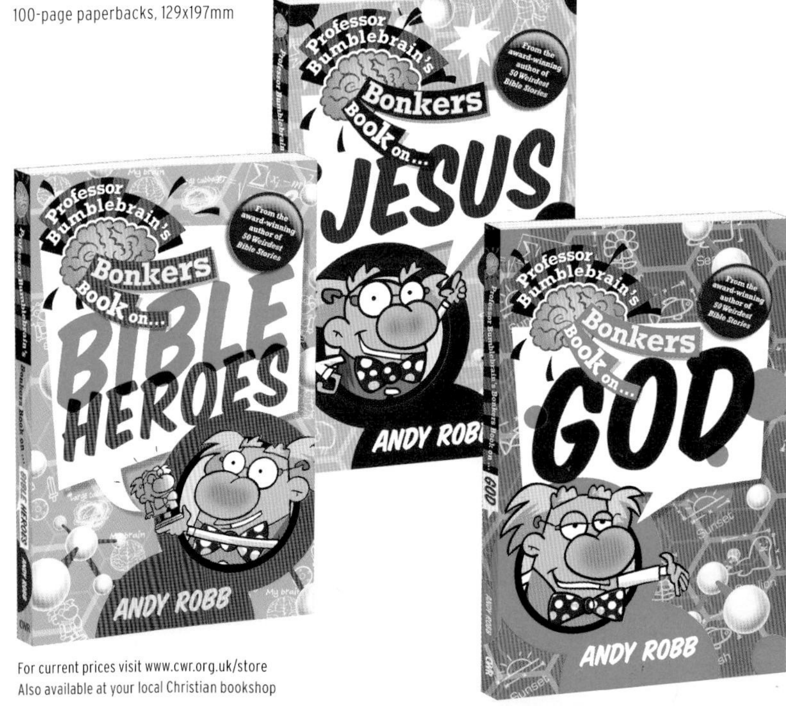

For current prices visit www.cwr.org.uk/store
Also available at your local Christian bookshop

More from Andy Robb!

The Bible is not an easy book to understand if you don't know where to start.

That's why Andy Robb has picked out some of the most exciting stories for you and told them in his own wacky way - which certainly won't leave you bored!

Each story has a cliffhanger ending - and a short Bible passage to look up so you can find out what happened next.

112-page paperbacks, 197x129mm

50 Goriest Bible Stories
Cain and Abel, Abraham and Isaac, Moses and his rebellious relations, David and Goliath, Judas and more.
ISBN: 978-1-85345-530-8

50 Weirdest Bible Stories
The Red Sea crossing, Jesus heals a paralysed man, manna in the desert, the dreams of Joseph, Peter walking on water and more.
ISBN: 978-1-85345-489-9

50 Wildest Bible Stories
Ruth and Boaz, Samson killing a lion with his bare hands, the Queen of Sheba's visit to Solomon, Jesus' temptation by Satan, Paul's angelic visit onboard a ship and more.
ISBN: 978-1-85345-529-2

50 Craziest Bible Stories
Jonah and the big fish, Elijah and the prophets of Baal, Balaam and the donkey, the feeding of the 5,000, Jesus' resurrection, the beggar at the Beautiful Gate and more.
ISBN: 978-1-85345-490-5